A Year to Rem...

19__3

For Those Whose Hearts Belong to 1963

Celebrating your year

1963

A memorable year for

Contents

Chapter 5: Iconic Moments in Entertainment

Chapter 6: The World Through the Eyes of 1963

Chapter 7: Iconic Advertisements of 1963

Introduction

A Year to Remember - 1963
For Those Whose Hearts Belong to 1963

To our cherished readers who hold a special connection to the year 1963, whether it's because you were born in this remarkable year, celebrated a milestone, or hold dear memories from that time, this book is a tribute to you and your unique connection to an unforgettable era.

In the pages that follow, we invite you to embark on a captivating journey back to 1963, a year of profound historical significance. For those with a personal connection to this year, it holds a treasure trove of memories, stories, and experiences that shaped the world and touched your lives.

Throughout this book, we've woven together the tapestry of 1963, providing historical insights, personal stories, and interactive activities that allow you to relive and celebrate the significance of this special year.

As you turn the pages and immerse yourself in the events and culture of 1963, we hope you'll find moments of nostalgia, inspiration, and the opportunity to rekindle cherished memories of this extraordinary year.

This book is dedicated to you, our readers, who share a unique bond with 1963. May it bring you joy, enlightenment, and a deeper connection to the rich tapestry of history that weaves through your lives.

With warm regards,
Erward Art Lab

Chapter 1: The Year That Changed America

1.1 Introduction to 1963

In the early 1960s, America was a country going through big changes. People were demanding fairness and equality for all, no matter their skin color. This year, 1963, became a turning point in American history. It was a year filled with hope, courage, and sorrow. Let's take a closer look at the events that made 1963 so significant.

1.2 The Civil Rights Movement

Imagine a time when people were treated differently because of their skin color. This was called segregation, and it was unfair. But in 1963, many brave people stood up to change this. African Americans, along with people of all races, joined together to fight for civil rights. They wanted equal treatment under the law and an end to discrimination.

1.3 The March on Washington for Jobs and Freedom (Washington, D.C.)

Following President Kennedy's civil rights address in June, SCLC leaders plan a mass action of national scale designed to ensure passage of civil rights legislation. Drawing together tens of thousands of Movement allies from across the nation – workers with SNCC, CORE, NAACP, and SCLC, as well as members of labor unions, interdenominational organizations, and student groups—the August 28 march from the Washington monument to the Lincoln memorial is the largest demonstration of its kind in history.

Over 200,000 people, black and white, gathered for the March on Washington for Jobs and Freedom. They wanted jobs, freedom, and an end to segregation. The highlight of the day was a powerful speech by Dr. Martin Luther King Jr.

1.4 Dr. Martin Luther King Jr.'s "I Have a Dream" Speech

Dr. King was a leader in the Civil Rights Movement. On that historic day, he stood in front of the Lincoln Memorial and spoke about his dream for a better America. He talked about a world where people would be judged by their character, not their skin color. His words still inspire us today.

"I HAVE A DREAM
THAT ONE DAY
THIS NATION WILL RISE UP
AND LIVE OUT
THE TRUE MEANING
OF IT'S CREED -
WE HOLD THESE TRUTHS
TO BE SELF-EVIDENT:
THAT ALL MEN
ARE CREATED EQUAL."

"I say to you today, my friends, so even though we face the difficulties of today and tomorrow, I still have a dream. It is a dream deeply rooted in the American dream."

1.5 JFK's Presidency and Assassination

On November 22, 1963, President John F. Kennedy was assassinated in Dallas, Texas, during a motorcade. He had been preparing for his re-election campaign, touring various states and addressing key themes. The Texas trip aimed to unite the Democratic Party and address political tensions in the state.

President John F. Kennedy reaches out to the crowd gathered at the Hotel Texas parking lot rally in Fort Worth, Texas

In Fort Worth, he spoke about national defense and the economy, receiving a warm reception. The next day, as he passed through Dealey Plaza in Dallas, shots were fired, fatally injuring President Kennedy and Governor John Connally. President Kennedy was pronounced dead at Parkland Memorial Hospital, and Vice President Lyndon B. Johnson was sworn in on Air Force One.

Lee Harvey Oswald, an employee at the Texas School Book Depository, was arrested for the assassination but was killed by Jack Ruby on live TV. President Kennedy's funeral, attended by world leaders, took place at Arlington National Cemetery, where an eternal flame was lit. His legacy continued to inspire hope, as he had urged in his inaugural address.

Arrival of President John F. Kennedy's casket at the White House.

Members of the Kennedy family, officials, and dignitaries attend graveside services in the state funeral of President John F. Kennedy

Chapter 1 takes us on a journey through the year 1963, a year that shaped America in profound ways. It shows how people fought for their rights, how Dr. Martin Luther King Jr. inspired a nation, and how the loss of President JFK touched the hearts of many. This chapter reminds us of the courage and challenges of that unforgettable year.

Activity:

"Today I tell you, my friends, that even though we face the difficulties of today and tomorrow, I still have a dream. It is a dream deeply rooted in American dream."

Whose famous quote is this?

A. John F. Kennedy

B. Mary Quant

C. Michael Jordan

D. Dr. Martin Luther King Jr.'s

Activity:
"Fill in the Blank - 1963 Events"

Instructions:

Fill in the blanks in the following sentences with the correct information about key events from 1963, as discusse in Chapter 1. Refer to the chapter for details.

Events:

1. In 1963, a significant event that took place in the Unite States was the _____.

2. The _____ was a pivotal movement that occurred throughout the year, marked by protests, sit-ins, and marches in the fight for civil rights.

3. On August 28, 1963, a historic gathering known as the _____ was held in Washington, D.C., where Dr. Martin Luther King Jr. delivered his iconic "I Have a Dream" speech.

4. Dr. Martin Luther King Jr.'s "I Have a Dream" speech advocated for _____ and justice, and it was delivered on the steps of the Lincoln Memorial.

5. The year 1963 also saw the presidency of _____, who had a significant impact on the United States.

6. Tragically, President Kennedy's life was cut short when he was assassinated on _____ in Dallas Texas.

Chapter 2: World in Motion
The Crucial Year of 1963

1963 was a year of global turbulence and transformation. The Cold War kept the world on edge, while space exploration soared to new heights. The Great Train Robbery added intrigue to the headlines, and the arrival of The Beatles on American shores marked a cultural revolution. This chapter explores a world in flux, where the balance of power, the boundaries of Earth, and the sounds of a new generation were all shifting.

2.1 The Cold War and Cuban Missile Crisis

The Cold War was a period of intense tension and rivalry between the United States and the Soviet Union that lasted for decades after World War II. These two superpowers didn't engage in direct military conflict but were engaged in a global struggle for influence and ideological dominance.

Cuban Missile Crisis

One of the most critical moments of the Cold War was the Cuban Missile Crisis in 1962. It began when the U.S. discovered that the Soviet Union was secretly placing nuclear missiles in Cuba, which is just 90 miles from Florida. This was a direct threat to U.S. security.

In response, the U.S. imposed a naval blockade around Cuba to prevent more missile shipments. For nearly two weeks, the world watched anxiously as tensions escalated. The U.S. and the Soviet Union were on the brink of nuclear war.

However, through intense negotiations and diplomatic efforts, both sides eventually reached an agreement. The Soviets agreed to remove their missiles from Cuba, and the U.S. pledged not to invade Cuba and also removed its missiles from Turkey.

The Cuban Missile Crisis is often considered one of the closest moments the world came to a nuclear war during the Cold War. It highlighted the dangers of nuclear weapons and the importance of diplomacy in preventing catastrophic conflicts. It also led to increased efforts to control nuclear arms and reduce the risk of a similar crisis in the future.

The New York Times.

LATE CITY EDITION

U.S. IMPOSES ARMS BLOCKADE ON CUBA ON FINDING OFFENSIVE-MISSILE SITES; KENNEDY READY FOR SOVIET SHOWDOWN

U.S. JUDGES GIVEN Chinese Open New Front; SHIPS MUST STOP
POWER TO REQUIRE Use Tanks Against Indians
VOTE FOR NEGROES

PRESIDENT GRAVE
Asserts Russians Lied and Put Hemisphere in Great Danger

The Washington Post

Kennedy Sees Basis for Cuba Talks
In K Plan If Missiles Are Removed;
Photo Plane Missing on Isle Flight

The New York Times.

U.S. IMPOSES ARMS BLOCKADE ON CUBA ON FINDING OFFENSIVE-MISSILE SITES; KENNEDY READY FOR SOVIET SHOWDOWN

The New York Times.

SOME SOVIET SHIPS SAID TO VEER FROM CUBA;
KHRUSHCHEV SUGGESTS A SUMMIT MEETING;
THANT BIDS U.S. AND RUSSIA DESIST 2 WEEKS

The New York Times.

KENNEDY AGREES TO TALKS ON THANT PLAN,
KHRUSHCHEV ACCEPTS IT; BLOCKADE GOES ON;
RUSSIAN TANKER INTERCEPTED AND CLEARED

The New York Times.

U.S. FINDS CUBA SPEEDING BUILD-UP OF BASES;
WARNS OF FURTHER ACTION; U.N. TALKS OPEN;
SOVIET AGREES TO SHUN BLOCKADE ZONE NOW

The New York Times.

GETS SOVIET OFFER TO END CUBA BASES,
ACCEPTS BID TO LINK IT TO THOSE IN TURKEY;
MOST ON PATROL, OTHER CRAFT FIRED ON

The New York Times.

U.S. AND SOVIET REACH ACCORD ON CUBA;
KENNEDY ACCEPTS KHRUSHCHEV PLEDGE
TO REMOVE MISSILES UNDER U.N. WATCH

The Washington Post FINAL

Reds Still Building Missile Sites; U. S. Insists They Be Eliminated

John Steinbeck Awarded the Nobel Prize

FINAL

DAILY NEWS

NEW YORK'S PICTURE NEWSPAPER

5¢

WE BLOCKADE CUBA ARMS

Red Ships Face Search or Sinking

17

2.2 The Space Race: America's First Woman in Space
The Space Race Takes Flight

Valentina Tereshkova became the first woman to travel to space on June 16, 1963, when she orbited Earth as part of the Vostok 6 mission. Tereshkova spent almost three days in space during her solo mission.She remains the youngest woman to fly to space, the only female astronaut or cosmonaut to make a solo space journey, and the first civilian to journey to space.

Valentina Tereshkova

Following her one and only space mission, Tereshkova has received a number of prestigious medals and has held many political positions, according to the Royal Museum of Greenwich. She has also toured the world as an advocate for Soviet science.

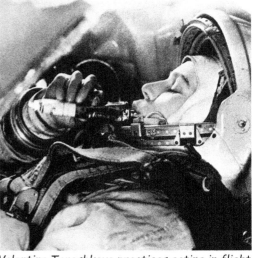

Valentina Tereshkova practices eating in flight simulations for launch into space.

Famous quotes from Valentina Tereshkova

"A bird cannot fly with one wing only. Human spaceflight cannot develop any further without the active participation of women."

"If women can be railroad workers in Russia, why can't they fly in space?"

"Once you've been in space, you appreciate how small and fragile the Earth is."

"Anyone who has spent any time in space will love it for the rest of their lives. I achieved my childhood dream of the sky."

"They forbade me from flying, despite all my protests and arguments. After being once in space, I was keen to go back there. But it didn't happen."

2.3 The Great Train Robbery in England

What was the Great Train Robbery?

On August 8, 1963, 15 men planned and executed a heist on a Royal Mail train carrying millions in cash.

Standing in wait for the train to pass Bridego Bridge, north of London, the robbers changed the green track signal to red using batteries, bringing the train to a halt.

When co-driver David Whitby went to investigate, he was thrown over the railway embankment. Meanwhile, the driver of the train, Jack Mills, was hit around the head and knocked unconscious.

The gang fled the scene within 30 minutes, taking 128 sacks with them.

Who was involved in the Great Train Robbery?

Those connected to the train robbery were a 15-strong gang of thieves, crooks and conspirers.

The most famous member is Ronnie Biggs, who escaped from London's Wandsworth prison in 1965.

Bruce Reynolds planned the robbery and, as a result, has become one of the most notorious criminals in British history.

Ronnie Biggs was jailed for 30 years for his part in the Great Train Robbery and was one of four prisoners that escaped from Wandsworth prison

How much did the robbers steal?

The robbers escaped with an estimated £2.6 million, which would have been worth about £46 million today, which they split amongst themselves.

Most of the cash has never been recovered.

What happened to the Great Train Robbers?
Most of them have now died.

Biggs decided to return to Britain to face arrest after becoming very ill. He died in December 2013 at a care home in East Barnet, London.

After being released from prison, Reynolds published Autobiography of a Thief in 1995 before dying in February 2013.

Edwards returned to selling flowers outside Waterloo station after being released but was found hanged in 1994.

Challenge time!

1. What was the most famous robbery in 1963?

A. Train Robbery in England
B. Ship Robbery in England
C. Space ship Robbery in England
D. House Robbery in England

2. You can ask this question to your children and grandchildren, so they can look it up with you and give the best answer!

_____

_____

_____

_____

_____

_____

_____

_____

_____

_____

3. What nationality was the first person to fly into space?

A. American
B. Vietnamese
C. Soviet Union
D. Russian

4. Let's draw it! Complete the picture by connecting consecutive numbers

Cold War Word Search

Instructions:

Search for the words related to the Cold War and its key players in the grid below. Circle each word as you find it. Words can appear horizontally, vertically, diagonally, and even backward.

Word List:

Kennedy	Berlin	Cold War	Espionage
Khrushchev	Soviet	Space Race	Arms Race
Cuba	United States	Alliance	Iron Curtain
Missile	Nuclear	Blockade	Cuban
Crisis	Tensions	Superpowers	Revolution
			Diplomacy

Word Search Grid:

```
U  A  J  K  M  S  V  E  S  P  I  O  N  A  G  E
T  N  N  I  C  X  D  P  B  C  E  Y  H  N  S  R
E  L  I  P  R  Q  X  C  L  U  P  Z  J  W  P  B
N  I  K  T  K  O  S  D  O  B  B  F  S  U  A  C
S  A  S  G  E  R  N  E  C  A  Y  E  X  F  T  J
I  N  R  A  E  D  E  C  K  W  H  U  R  Q  Z  N
O  C  Q  M  Y  S  S  J  U  K  F  I  S  L  C  Q
N  E  M  O  G  I  N  T  D  R  Z  I  A  J  I  L
S  K  C  I  B  S  E  A  A  S  T  D  U  T  X  N
P  C  U  B  A  N  R  E  V  O  L  U  T  I  O  N
L  O  W  C  L  S  Y  L  G  E  E  T  I  Y  V  F
B  F  K  H  R  U  S  H  C  H  E  S  H  N  L  W
B  C  W  F  Z  N  W  L  A  R  M  S  E  A  C  E
C  E  Q  E  R  K  C  A  E  W  U  B  E  R  A  D
S  O  V  I  E  T  Q  E  R  Y  B  E  D  S  S  O
Z  U  D  P  Y  P  D  I  P  L  O  M  A  C  Y  U
```

Chapter 3: Cultural Milestones

Cultural Revolution

The cultural milestones of 1963 show us a society in transition. Music was evolving with the arrival of The Beatles. Television provided a window into both rural America and the world of the ultra-rich. Toys like the Hula Hoop brought joy to the young and the young at heart. And fashion, with the mini-skirt, was breaking new ground. This chapter captures the spirit of a changing culture, where entertainment, fashion, and trends were shaping the way people lived and thought.

3.1 The Beatles conquer the world

In 1963, the Beatles were exploding in England. Their debut LP, Please Please Me, came out in March, followed by their megahit single "She Loves You" in August. Their second album, With the Beatles, and another hit single, "I Want to Hold Your Hand," followed in the fall. Screaming girls, throngs of fans, bushels of albums being sold—this was when it all started

The Beatles

I WANT TO HOLD YOUR HAND
THIS BOY

Parlophone
R 5084

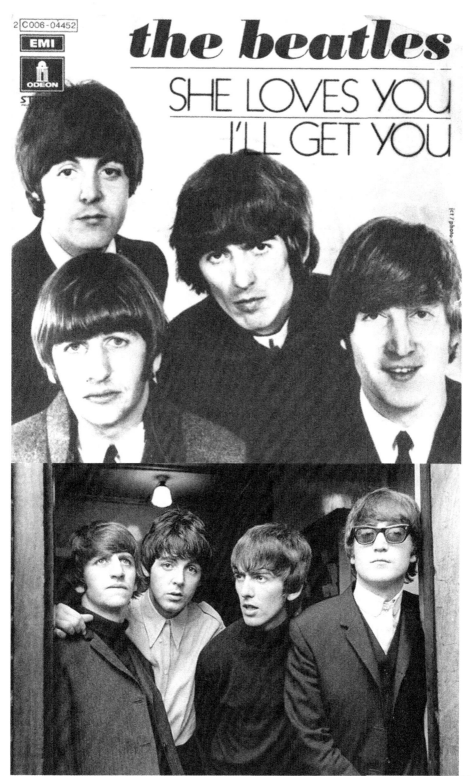

2 C006-04452

EMI

ODEON

the beatles

SHE LOVES YOU
I'LL GET YOU

The Beatles 1963

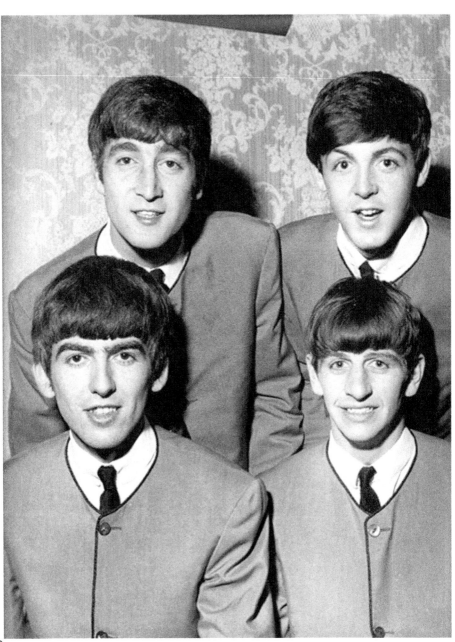

3.2 The Popularity of TV Shows like "The Andy Griffith Show" and "The Beverly Hillbillies"

Television was a big part of American life in 1963, and two shows in particular captured the hearts of viewers. "The Andy Griffith Show" charmed audiences with its small-town humor and lovable characters. "The Beverly Hillbillies" tickled funny bones with the adventures of a hillbilly family suddenly thrust into Beverly Hills luxury.

Television Classic

The Beverly Hillbillies

It was more than just a sitcom; it was a reflection of the American fascination with wealth and the enduring appeal of characters who stay true to themselves, no matter where life takes them. In 1963, it was a ratings juggernaut, and its humor and heart continue to entertain audiences today. This chapter celebrates the hilarious escapades of the Clampett family and the enduring legacy of "The Beverly Hillbillies."

Cast:The main cast included Buddy Ebsen as Jed Clampett, Irene Ryan as Granny, Max Baer Jr. as Jethro Bodine, and Donna Douglas as Ellie Mae Clampett. The characters brought a unique blend of country charm and fish-out-of-water comedy to the series.

Audience and Popularity: "The Beverly Hillbillies" was an instant hit and consistently ranked as one of the top-rated shows on television during its run. In 1963, it reached a wide and enthusiastic audience, becoming a cultural phenomenon.

Themes and Humor: The show used humor to comment on societal norms and values, often highlighting the absurdities of materialism and social status. The characters' rural innocence contrasted sharply with the extravagance of Beverly Hills, leading to many comedic situations.

The Andy Griffith Show

It was more than just a comedy. It was a reflection of the values of small-town America in the 1960s. The show emphasized the importance of community, friendship, and doing the right thing. It used humor and heart to teach life lessons that resonated with viewers of all ages. "The Andy Griffith Show" was a beloved American sitcom that aired from 1960 to 1968, and it was indeed in its prime during the year 1963.

Setting and Characters: The show was set in the fictional small town of Mayberry, North Carolina, and revolved around the life of Sheriff Andy Taylor, played by Andy Griffith. The show featured a memorable cast of characters, including Barney Fife (played by Don Knotts), Opie Taylor (played by Ron Howard), Aunt Bee (played by Frances Bavier), and many more.

Plot and Themes: "The Andy Griffith Show" was known for its wholesome and family-friendly humor. It often explored moral lessons and values while highlighting the simple pleasures of life in a tight-knit community. Sheriff Andy Taylor, with his wisdom and patience, served as a father figure to his son Opie and his bumbling but well-meaning deputy, Barney Fife.

Popularity: In 1963, the show was at the height of its popularity. It consistently ranked among the top-rated television programs during its run. Audiences across the United States embraced the show's heartwarming stories and endearing characters.

In 1963, "The Andy Griffith Show" was a staple of American television, providing viewers with wholesome entertainment and a charming glimpse into the life of Mayberry.

The Best Songs From 1963
1. Surfin' U.S.A. - The Beach Boys

Surfin' U.S.A. is actually a rewritten version of Chuck Berry's Sweet Little Sixteen, with completely new lyrics laid over the same tune. It served as the opening title track of The Beach Boys' 1963 album and was almost emblematic of the California Sound we know today. It was also the biggest hit of the year in 1963, launching them even further into stardom and cementing their place as one of the most iconic groups of all time.

2. The End Of The World – Skeeter Davis

The End Of The World was written by Arthur Kent and Sylvia Davis for Skeeter Davis, and her recording of the song was again one of the biggest hits of the year in 1963. Likening the climactic end of a relationship to a literal apocalypse of the heart, the track quickly rose on the US charts to peak at number two on the Hot 100. It then went on to become a top-five hit on other US charts, including the Easy Listening, R&B, and Hot Country Singles rankings.

4. He's So Fine - The ChiffonsIpsum

He's So Fine turned out to be a big hit single for several different artists, but the first and most successful version of the track was recorded by The Chiffons. Theirs is still one of the most recognizable oldies songs in existence and was the renowned track in the famous plagiarism case against George Harrison's My Sweet Lord single.

5. Blue Velvet - Bobby Vinton

Blue Velvet was inspired by a trip to the Jefferson Hotel in Richmond Virginia and was originally written by Bernie Wayne in the 50s. The first version of the song came from Tony Bennet who scored a top-20 hit with it. Among the other tracks on this list, this one may be the most record-ed single, but it was Bobby Vinto who found the most success with it. In 1963, his version of the song rose to the top of the Hot 100 and Cash Box Top 100 charts.

Musical Highlights And Achievements

- **Vaughn Meader Stuns:** A relatively unknown comic, Vaughn Meader, took home the Album of the Year for The First Family, a comedy album parodying President Kennedy.

- **Tony Bennett's Big Night**: Tony Bennett won Record of the Year for I Left My Heart in San Francisco, which became one of his signature songs.

- **Pioneering Female Award**: The first Best Female Pop Vocal Performance went to Ella Fitzgerald for Ella Swings Brightly with Nelson.

- **Classical Milestone**: Leonard Bernstein won multiple awards for his conducting, solidifying his place in classical music history.

Share your 1963 photos,

Don't forget to show off your fabulous '60s fashion!

Activity:
Relax with tic-tac-toe

The winner has the right to ask 5 questions related to the opponent's life and knowledge about the year 1963. If the winner was born in 1963, congratulate them on their birthday and sing the happy birthday song together.

Chapter 4: Sports in 1963

Sporting Highlights for 1963

Margaret Court won the Australian Open for the fourth straight time which was also her sixth grand slam win. Margaret also won her first Wimbledon title that year. She would go on to win the Australian Open seven more times and the Wimbledon two more times en-route to a career with 24 grand slam titles.

Roy Emerson won the Australian Open for the second time, which he would win four more times for a total of six Australian Open titles and a total of 12 grand slam titles.

Jack Nicklaus, who already had a major win under his belt, won two majors, the Masters Tournament and the PGA Championship that year. Julius Boros won the U.S. Open for the second time.

Mickey Wright, who is one of the most accomplished golfers in the LPGA, won two majors, the Women's Western Open and the LPGA Championship for her 10th and 11th major titles. Mary Mills and Marilynn Smith, both with multiple major wins, won the U.S. Women's Open and the Titleholders Championship respectively for their first major title.

In Formula One, **Jim Clark** won seven races for his first driver's championship by a 21 point margin. Clark also won the Championship again for the second and last time in 1965.

Jacques Anquetil of France, one of the three riders ever to win the Tour de France five times won the race for the fourth straight year.

Below is a timeline of some significant results in the world of sport for the year 1963

Date	Results
Jan	Tennis Australia Open won by Roy Emerson and Margaret Smith
April	Golf Masters won by Jack Nicklaus (1st win)
May	Tennis French Open won by Roy Emerson and Lesley Turner
June	Golf US Open won by Julius Boros
July	the Cycling Tour de France won by Jacques Anquetil
July	Tennis Wimbledon won by Chuck McKinley and Margaret Smith
July	Golf The Open Championship won by Bob Charles
Aug	Golf US PGA won by Jack Nicklaus
Sep	Tennis US National Championship won by Rafael Osuna and Maria Bueno
Oct	The Baseball World Series won by Los Angeles Dodgers

4.2 The Tragedy of Fireball Roberts: A Loss for NASCAR

In 1963, the world of NASCAR racing suffered a devastating loss with the passing of Glenn "Fireball" Roberts. Fireball was a beloved and accomplished driver known for his skill and his fiery personality. Tragedy struck during a race at the Charlotte Motor Speedway in North Carolina.

Although the accident occurred in 1963, Fireball Roberts succumbed to his injuries in July 1964, leaving the racing world in mourning. His legacy as a fearless racer and fan favorite endures, serving as a reminder of the risks and the deep bonds within the NASCAR community

Activity: "1963 Sports Event Match-Up"

Instructions:

Match the correct sports event with its respective winner from the list of significant sporting achievements in 1963. Write the letter corresponding to the correct winner next to the event.

Sports Events:

Tennis Australia Open
Golf Masters
Tennis French Open
Golf US Open
Cycling Tour de France
Tennis Wimbledon
Golf The Open Championship
Golf US PGA
Tennis US National Championship
Baseball World Series

Possible Winners:

A. Roy Emerson
B. Margaret Smith
C. Jack Nicklaus
D. Julius Boros
E. Jacques Anquetil
F. Chuck McKinley
G. Bob Charles
H. Rafael Osuna
I. Maria Bueno
J. Los Angeles Dodgers

Match-Up:

1. Tennis Australia Open: _____
2. Golf Masters: _____
3. Tennis French Open: _____
4. Golf US Open: _____
5. Cycling Tour de France: _____
6. Tennis Wimbledon: _____
7. Golf The Open Championship: _____
8. Golf US PGA: _____
9. Tennis US National Championship: _____
10. Baseball World Series: _____

Chapter 5: Iconic Moments in Entertainment

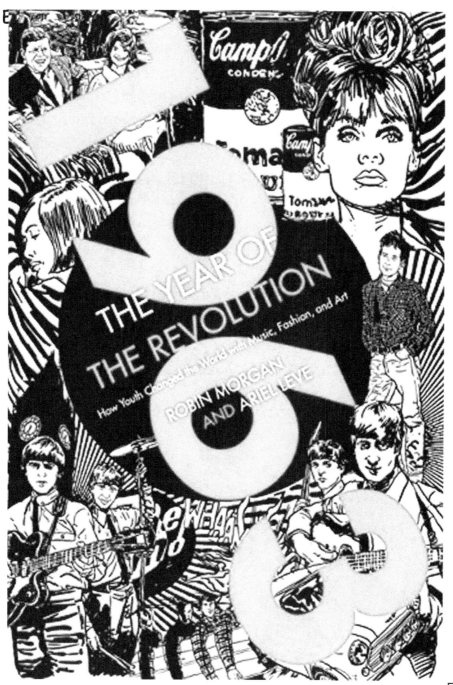

1963 was a year that left an indelible mark on the world of entertainment. From Hitchcock's spine-tingling "The Birds" to the time-traveling adventures of "Doctor Who," the celebration of the performing arts at The Kennedy Center Honors, and the groundbreaking introduction of the X-Men, these moments in entertainment have continued to shape our culture and captivate audiences for generations. This chapter celebrates the enduring impact of these iconic moments in the world of entertainment.

5.1 The Release of Alfred Hitchcock's "The Birds"

In 1963, legendary filmmaker Alfred Hitchcock unleashed a cinematic masterpiece that would ruffle feathers and chill spines— "The Birds." This suspenseful thriller brought to life the terrifying idea of birds turning against humans in a small California town.

"It could be the most terrifying motion picture I have ever made!"—

NOTHING YOU HAVE EVER WITNESSED BEFORE HAS PREPARED YOU FOR SUCH SHEER STABBING SHOCK!

ALFRED HITCHCOCK'S "The Birds"
TECHNICOLOR

Starring Tippi Hedren and Rod Taylor, "The Birds" created suspense like no other. The film's eerie atmosphere and unforgettable scenes of avian terror left audiences on the edge of their seats. It became a classic in the realm of suspense and remains a spine-tingling experience for viewers to this day.

5.2 The Premiere of "Doctor Who"

On November 23, 1963, a new era in science fiction television began with the premiere of "Doctor Who" on the BBC. This groundbreaking series introduced the enigmatic Time Lord known as the Doctor, who traveled through time and space in the TARDIS, a time machine that looked like a British police box.

"Doctor Who" quickly became a cultural phenomenon, captivating audiences with its inventive storytelling and memorable characters. The Doctor's ability to regenerate allowed different actors to portray the character over the years, ensuring the show's longevity and cementing its place as a beloved part of British television history.

5.3 The Launch of the X-Men Comic Series: Superheroes with a Twist

In September 1963, Marvel Comics introduced the world to a group of mutants with extraordinary abilities—the X-Men. Created by writer Stan Lee and artist Jack Kirby, the X-Men were a team of superheroes who faced prejudice and discrimination because of their unique powers.

What set the X-Men apart was their relatability and complexity. They grappled with societal issues and were often seen as outsiders. This comic series, which began in 1963, would go on to spawn a vast universe of characters and become one of Marvel's most iconic franchises.

The X-Men, also known as the "Children of the Atom," were a group of mutants, individuals born with genetic mutations that granted them superhuman powers. However, these mutations often made them outsiders in society.

The original X-Men team consisted of five members: Professor Charles Xavier (Professor X), Cyclops, Marvel Girl (Jean Grey), Beast, and Iceman.

Superhero Action with a Twist:

The X-Men comics featured the action-packed adventures and battles against supervillains that were typical of superhero comics. However, they also delved into the personal struggles and ethical dilemmas faced by the mutant heroes.

Each X-Man had unique powers and personalities. Cyclops could emit powerful optic blasts, Jean Grey possessed telekinetic and telepathic abilities, Beast had superhuman agility and strength, and Iceman could create ice and freeze objects.

The Villains:

The X-Men faced a wide range of adversaries, including the Brotherhood of Evil Mutants led by Magneto, who believed in mutant superiority, and the Sentinels, giant mutant-hunting robots.

Evolution and Expansion:

The X-Men comic series continued to evolve and expand, introducing new characters like Wolverine, Storm, Night-crawler, and Colossus, who would become iconic members of the X-Men.

The stories explored complex relationships within the team, including the on-again, off-again romance between Cyclops and Jean Grey.

58

Celebrities Born In 1963

This is a shout-out to my favorite celebrities who were born in 1963.

- **George Michael** June 25th. Which also happens to be my birthday. Which makes George my birthday buddy.
- **Michael Jordan** February 17th. The King of the Court. Also my favorite basketball player.
- **Johnny Depp** June 9th. JD is my favorite actor. There isn't a movie that Johnny starred in that I didn't like.
- **Brad Pitt** December 18th. The other half of Brangelina since he hooked up with Angelina Jolie.
- **Mike Myers** May 25th. Mike starred in some of my favorite movies. Wayne's World, Austin Powers and Shrek.
- **John Stamos** August 19th. Since he started on Full House as Jesse Katsopolis he's gained many fans who continue to follow his career.
- **Helen Hunt** June 15th. From Twister, Cast Away, Pay It Forward to As Good As It Gets...Helen just keeps getting better with each role she stars in.
- **Travis Tritt** February 9th. Country music wouldn't be the same without Travis and his twangy hits.
- **Lisa Kudrow** July 30th. What would Friends have been without Phoebe Buffay and her many hysterical antics.
- **Jennifer Beals** December 19th. If you are a fan of the movie Flashdance, you'll remember Jennifer.
- **Conan O'Brien** April 18th. American talk show host.

Activity:

Please color this picture!

Chapter 6: The World Through the Eyes of 1963

6.1 Fashion Trends and Fads
Vintage 1963 Fashion including Dusters, Slacks, Suits, Capris, Pants and Dresses

1963 A-Line Duster A-Line Duster Description Wear it flowing in the smart A-line or cinch it with the self fabric rope belt for that classic wrap around look. Extra points include two handy side seam pockets, set in sleeves for a smooth shoulder line. Smart collarless styling, six button closing. Fine pinwale cotton corduroy. Colors are red or blue.

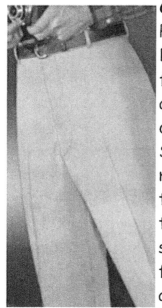

Combed Cotton Slacks
Price: $5.00
Description Because of it's extra-long fibers this wears longer, yet is softer and more silk-like in appearance than ordinary cotton. It is mercerized and Sanforized-Plus protected which means it is proven wash and wear. Its texture is smooth because it is so tightly woven.The youthful campus styling has no-pleat front. Choose from tan, charcoal gray, bone white, and dark olive green.

All In One Insulated Suit
Price: $17.90
Description   All-in-one suit is nylon lined and has a bi-swing pleated back. Front zipper opens at top and bottom. Two roomy back pockets, one with zipper closing. Self belt. Mercerized cotton knit wristlets. Neat pants bottoms, no cuffs. Comes in spruce green or charcoal gray.

Capri Outfit
Price: $5.83
Description   Cotton corduroy capri outfit has a pull-on overblouse with a bold collar, tassel-trimmed front   and   back. Three-quarter   length sleeves, side vents. Pants have hi-rise waist and back zipper. Colors are bright teal blue and black.

Checked Wool Stretch Pants
Price: $9.83
Description Checked wool and stretch nylon, woven in black and white. Pants have side zipper and contour stirrups.

Cotton Corduroy Maternity Wear
Price: $3.89 - $4.89
Description White combed cotton blouse ($3.89) has a detachable bow and button front. Printed cotton corduroy popover top ($4.89) has an abstract design and button-trimmed open side vents, colors are red, green and beige print or moss green, turquoise blue and light green print. Cotton corduroy capri pants ($3.89) are made with a Helanca nylon yarn stretch front panel and come in red or moss green.

Demi Jacketed Dress
Price: $27.50
Description Demi-jacketed dress is made with lustrous acetate satin that is artfully dotted with beading. Bare shoulder dress is back zippered and the shell jacket has three back fasteners. Bell-shaped skirt is Pellon lined to keep its shape. Colors are gold or turquoise.

Cotton Oxford Step In Dress
Price: $5.84

Description Cotton oxford-cloth step-in dress buttons to the waistline. Colors are dark loden green or rust brown.

Double Fur Collar Stole
Price: $595.00

Description Natural mink fully let-out to reveal its depth and irresistible beauty. Back is about eighteen inches deep; length from center back to front tip is about thirty inches. Silk and rayon lining. Comes in Cerulean (blue-gray) or Tourmaline (pale beige).

Dramatic Gown
Price: $22.50

Description Dramatic gown has acetate and nylon lace and a nylon sheer cummerbund. Dress has nylon net petticoat and is lined in acetate taffeta. Colors are light rose, light blue or white.

Fine Line Gabardine Slacks
Price: $3.66
Description Fine line gabardine in continental style. Beltless, cuffless, low-riding. Inside waist tabs, smooth cotton with muted luster. Sanforized-plus finish for wrinkle-resistance during wear or in the wash. Colors are loden green, black or grayish brown.

Shaggy Mohair Sweater
Price: $12.77
Description The look of this coat sweater: shaggy. The fabric is made with seventy-five percent brushed mohair and twenty-five percent wool with suede leather trim. Comes in gray or light tan.

Men's Embroidered Shirts
Price: $3.80 - $4.80
Description Special styling creates this distinctive three-dimensional embroidery. So neat, so rich looking it resembles finest hand workmanship. Adds a rich elegance to these sport shirts. Regular spread top-stitched collar with permanent stays. Square-cut adjustable cuffs.

Whipcord Sport Suit
Price: $26.50
Description A hard finished rayon and acetate fabric in a subtle diagonal weave. Handsomely tailored along traditional lines and accented with a smart contrasting handkerchief in breast pocket that matches coat lining. Three-button coat with patch flap pockets, natural shoulders and hook vent back. Colorful rayon lining. With matching pointed model vest. Plain front trousers. Comes in black or dark olive.

Roman Coin Print Shirt
Price: $2.97
Description Roman coin print... so rich looking in wine red and brown on beige ground. Fashioned with a stylish mandarin-look collar and roll-up sleeves. Shirt-tail bottom for in or out versatility. It goes equally well with pants and skirts.

1963 Fashion Accessories

Bag and Glove Set

Price: $4.77
Description Bag and glove set is made with acetate satin. Gloves have nylon stretch palms and measure around eight inches long. Clutch bag is acetate lined. Comes in pink or white.

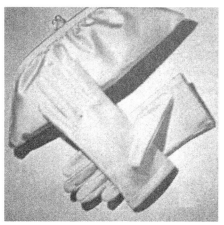

Crushable Dress Hat
Price: $10.70
Description Snaps back into shape when wrinkled-- you can even pack it in a suitcase. Lightweight fur felt body in center dent style-- factory pre-blocked. Form-ease reeded roan leather sweatband with "floating" construction for extra comfort. Hand felted edge on brim. Acetate taffeta lining with plio-film tipping. Rayon grosgrain ribbon band and bow. Colors are cinder gray, dark brown, and dusk gray

Buckle Oxford

Price: $9.77

Description Dashing new oxford has side strap and buckle. Soft, shiny black leather uppers have masculine hand-sewn front for greater flexibility. The lean, tapered-toe is squared at the tip. Sturdy rubber sole, hard heel. Really a fashionable addition to your shoe wardrobe.

Draped Turban

Price: $5.97

Description Draped turban made with rayon velvet. Has stick pin. Colors to choose from include red, black, dark brown or coffee brown.

Feather and Felt Pillbox

Price: $5.97

Description Pillbox hat made with fur felt. It has a large feather accent across the front. Hat comes in black, coffee brown, off-white or sapphire medium blue.

Red Crocodile Shoe and Bag

Price: $6.77, $12.97

Description Crocodile-grained calf pouch ($12.97) so very "now", yet forever fashionable with its timeless shaping and tasteful detailing. Crocodile-grained kidskin leather upper on pump ($6.77). Its crocodile look is artfully embossed to create high fashion excitement. Choose from cherry red, medium tan, or black.

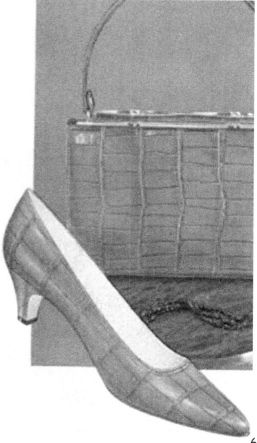

Roller Pillbox
Price: $4.97
Description Roller pillbox hat is made with velour fur felt and has a veil. Colors to choose from include blue, black, off-white or dark brown.

Long Leg Slimming Panty
Price: $9.80
Description Flexible boning for a firmer, leaner look. Satin elastic panels control tummy, back, hip and thigh. Power net body with easy-on side

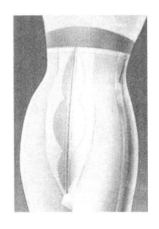

Satchel Pouch Price: $3.57
Description Satchel pouch, a "rough and ready" casual in textured jute cloth. Nicely trimmed with black plastic, saddle stitching and gold-color metal rings. Rayon lined. Comes in black or natural tan.zipper. Six hidden garters detach.

Share your 1963 photos,

Let us see the classic cars that were your pride and joy

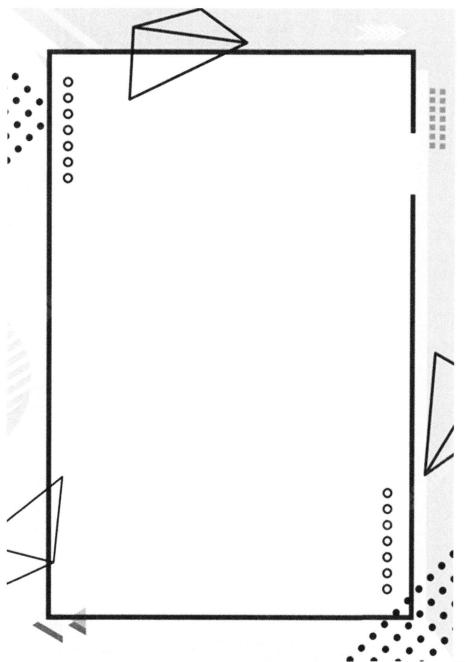

Activity

Color these outfits with your favorite colors!
Hey my designer! Let's color it

1960s Beach Time

PAPER THIN PERSONAS
Jewels &
Gemstones 2.0

1969

1965

1965

1965

1965

1965

1969

1961

1962

1965

Cut along dark lines and/or dotted lines. Mount or Print on Card.

1961

1965

1965

1965

1961

Amethyst

Swim Suit
1961

Due to this paper doll's historical underwear, some of the Jewels and Gemstones 2.0 paper doll clothing may not fit.

73

6.2 The cost of living in 1963

In 1963, money had a different purchasing power compared to today. Here are some examples of what you could buy with various amounts of money in the United States during that year:

Groceries:

- A loaf of bread: 22 cents
- A dozen eggs: 55 cents
- A gallon of milk: 49 cents
- A pound of ground beef: 39 cents

76

Transportation:

- A gallon of gasoline: 29 cents

- **A new car**: The average cost of a new car was around $3,233

Housing:

- Median home price: The median price for a new home

Entertainment:

Movie ticket: A movie ticket typically cost around $2.20

A paperback book: You could purchase a paperback book for $1 or less.

Electronics:

Color television set: Color TVs were still relatively new and expensive, costing several hundred dollars.

Education:

College tuition: The cost of college tuition varied, but on average, it was significantly lower than today's rates. Public university tuition was often a few hundred dollars per year.

Postage:
A stamp: 5 cents

Wages:
The average annual income for an American worker in 1963 was around $5,800.

Healthcare:
Doctor's office visit: A routine doctor's visit might cost around $5-$10

6.3 Popular Toys and Games

Children in 1963 had a wealth of new toys and games to enjoy. The Easy-Bake Oven, a miniature working oven for kids, was a sensation, allowing young chefs to bake tiny treats. Barbie dolls continued to be popular, with new outfits and accessories to collect.

Big Loo Moon Robot

Manufacturer: Marx
Price: $9.99
Description This Moon Robot is over three feet tall and says ten different things. One of his arms fires plastic balls and the other arm picks things up. His base launches rockets and has a compass, while his chest shoots darts and squirts water. He has lighted eyes that blink.

Bozo the Clown Talking Doll

Manufacturer:
Price: $5.77
Description Wears a blue and white polka dot suit and has rooted bright red hair. Pull his chatty ring to hear a number of phrases.

Casper the Ghost
Manufacturer: Mattel
Price: $5.99
Description This talking Casper the Ghost says one of eleven phrases every time you pull his chatty ring. He has a stuffed body covered with white rayon plush and a plastic face. As technology became cheaper Toys in the 1960s reflected this by becoming more interactive

Musical TV Phonograph
Manufacturer: Playskool
Price: $3.99
Description Listen to the music-box sound of "Skip to my Lou" and watch the children dancing happily on the revolving screen in bright colors. Comes with three records in storage slot.

Troll Dolls
Manufacturer:
Price: $1.44 each
Description These pot-bellied and bow-legged Trolls need you for a friend. Choose from Bride, Groom, Nurse, or Indian Chief.

Activity

Coloring time!

85

Chapter 7: Iconic advertisements

7.1 Marketing Masterpieces: Remembering Vintage Ads
Model-Year Madness! Classic Ads From 1963

Go great! Go Plymouth '63 . . . the happy-GO-liveliest car of the year! *And this one really goes!* Plymouth's like a tiger on the road the way it claws up the miles. Plymouth's a pure-bred beauty—it's longer, sleeker, slinkier. Grand on comfort. Great on ride. And engineered to go better than the rest with its 50,000 mile—5 year power-train warranty! What happens when you uncage this tiger just has to be called sensational. Fact is, it takes a Plymouth to catch a Plymouth!

'63 PLYMOUTH
the happy-GO-liveliest car of the year!

IT'S EXCITING!

'63 CHEVY II NOVA 4-DOOR SEDAN

GO '63 CHEVY II

Hard as it may be to believe, this year's Chevy II is better than last year's and better than anything in its class. It combines all of the new car-saving easy-care features of the big Chevrolet with its own wonderful attributes of parkable size, four- or six-cylinder fuel economy and interiors that'd do justice to cars that cost twice as much with half the charm. Last year Chevy II appeared and captured the public's fancy in no time at all . . . made a permanent place for itself with its sparkling performance and nickel-nursing economy. Yes sir, if you want maximum comfort and performance with minimum cash outlay and upkeep, you're talking about the Chevy II.

'63 CHEVY II NOVA 400 STATION WAGON

'63 CHEVY II NOVA 400 CONVERTIBLE

It's Chevy Showtime '63! – See the Go Show at Your Chevrolet Showroom

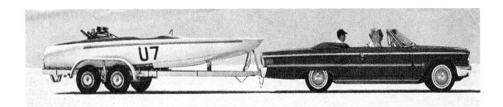

Q. Which dreamboat won the Orange Bowl Regatta?

A. The one with the <u>seagoing</u> Thunderbird V·8!

That salty winner being hoisted clear of the water is Mike Wallace's Tiny Tim, whose powerful Thunderbird engine proved too much for the 84 other ski boats in this year's Orange Bowl classic. On the road or planing over Miami's blue-green waters, Ford's mighty power plant is a tone poem of V-8 performance.

The landlocked vehicle is available with one of six Thunderbird V-8's from 164 to 425 horsepower. These strong, silent engines . . . when mated to one of four transmissions . . . make light work of those long portages between races. Ford's sturdy but supple rear leaf springs help make the Ford an outstanding tow car. Deep-foam bucket seats, and Ford's $10,000,000 ride, deliver captain and crew at the next launch site ready to show a clean white wake to the rest of the com-

petition. The way to go to the boat races, obviously, is with an all-Ford-powered rig . . . the way the winners do!

FOR 60 YEARS THE SYMBOL  MOTOR COMPANY
OF DEPENDABLE PRODUCTS

**If it's Ford-built, it's built for
performance . . . total performance**

FORD

FALCON · FAIRLANE · FORD · THUNDERBIRD

For 1963, Ford ads concentrated on selling all of its trucks

1963 Ford Falcon Sprint and Futura Convertibles

Need alley-oop?

It's yours with this quick, fresh lift!

Does that bowling ball feel heavier than it did a few minutes ago? Quick—bring on the 7-Up! Here's brand new energy for you in just 2 to 6 minutes. New roll-power to help you score bigger. New sparkle for your spirit. And a glorious, new, fresh taste for your mouth. Why, it's a bowler's dream. Or a ping ponger's. Or anybody's! It's *always* 7-Up time.

FOR THIRST QUENCHING, FRESH TASTE, QUICK LIFT..."FRESH UP" WITH SEVEN-UP!

7up 1963

AVON CALLING
makes the great difference

Your Avon Representative comes to you...that's one great difference. At home, at ease, blissfully relaxed, you choose cosmetics and fragrances of the finest quality that are just right for you. That's another great difference. Only your Avon Representative offers you this superb combination: this special joy of beauty, this rare joy of personal service. Consequently, Avon Calling is America's most popular way to select cosmetics.

Avon
cosmetics
RADIO CITY, NEW YORK
©1963 Avon Products, Inc.

1963 Avon

Oh! somewhere in this favored land the sun is shining bright

The band is playing somewhere, and somewhere hearts are light

And somewhere men are laughing, and somewhere children shout

But there is no joy in Mudville—for the Corn Flakes are fresh out

 CORN FLAKES

1963 Kellogg's Corn Flakes

For your Light-hearted moments...

1963 Supreme Chocolate Fudge Cookies advertisement

Add 5-Flavor variety to your dog's life
with *Walter Kendall.* **fives**

1963 Fives Dog Food

7.2 Pitch Perfect: Slogans That Stood the Test of Time
1. Coca-Cola - "Things Go Better with Coke"

Crowd cheers! Coke nears!
Game goes better refreshed
Coca-Cola, never too sweet,
gives that special zing ... refreshes best

This campaign emphasized the idea that Coca-Cola could enhance social interactions and everyday experiences, making them more enjoyable.

2. Winston Cigarettes - "Winston Tastes Good Like a Cigarette Should"

This slogan highlighted the taste and satisfaction of Winston cigarettes, positioning them as a preferred choice for smokers.

3. Pepsi - "Come Alive! You're in the Pepsi Generation"

Pepsi's campaign aimed to appeal to a younger and more vibrant audience, encouraging them to embrace the "Pepsi Generation" spirit.

Activity: "Slogan Match Up Challenge"

Instructions:

In this activity, readers will match the famous advertising slogans from 1963 with the respective brands or products they represent. Read the slogans and write down the corresponding brand or product name in the provided space.

Slogans:

1. "Things Go Better with Coke"
2. "Winston Tastes Good Like a Cigarette Should"
3. "Come Alive! You're in the Pepsi Generation"

Space for Matching:

1 - Brand/Product: _____

2 - Brand/Product: _____

3 - Brand/Product: _____

We have heartfelt thank-you gifts for you

As a token of our appreciation for joining us on this historical journey through 1963, we've included a set of cards and stamps inspired by the year of 1963. These cards are your canvas to capture the essence of the past. We encourage you to use them as inspiration for creating your own unique cards, sharing your perspective on the historical moments we've explored in this book. Whether it's a holiday greeting or a simple hello to a loved one, these cards are your way to connect with the history we've uncovered together.

Happy creating!

Activity answers

Chapter 1:

The quotes belong to Dr. Martin Luther King Jr.'s
Answers:

1. In 1963, a significant event that took place in the United States was the assassination of President John F. Kennedy.

2. The Civil Rights Movement was a pivotal movement that occurred throughout the year, marked by protests, sit-ins, and marches in the fight for civil rights.

3. On August 28, 1963, a historic gathering known as the March on Washington for Jobs and Freedom was held in Washington, D.C., where Dr. Martin Luther King Jr. delivered his iconic "I Have a Dream" speech.

4. Dr. Martin Luther King Jr.'s "I Have a Dream" speech advocated for racial equality and justice, and it was delivered on the steps of the Lincoln Memorial.

5. The year 1963 also saw the presidency of John F. Kennedy (JFK), who had a significant impact on the United States.

6. Tragically, President Kennedy's life was cut short when he was assassinated on November 22 in Dallas, Texas.

Chapter 2:

1.The most famous robbery in 1963 was the Train Robbery in England.
2. This question can indeed be a fun way to engage with family members and encourage them to explore historical events together.
3. The first person to fly into space was of Soviet Union nationality (Soviet cosmonaut Yuri Gagarin).

Chapter 4: Answers:

1. Tennis Australia Open: A (Roy Emerson) and B (Margaret Smith)
2. Golf Masters: C (Jack Nicklaus)
3. Tennis French Open: A (Roy Emerson)
4. Golf US Open: D (Julius Boros)
5. Cycling Tour de France: E (Jacques Anquetil)
6. Tennis Wimbledon: F (Chuck McKinley) and B (Margaret Smith)
7. Golf The Open Championship: G (Bob Charles)
8. Golf US PGA: C (Jack Nicklaus)
9. Tennis US National Championship: H (Rafael Osuna) and I (Maria Bueno)
10. Baseball World Series: J (Los Angeles Dodgers)

Chapter 7:

Things Go Better with Coke" - Brand/Product: Coca-Cola
"Winston Tastes Good Like a Cigarette Should" - Brand/Product: Winston Cigarettes
"Come Alive! You're in the Pepsi Generation" - Brand/Product: Pepsi

Embracing 1963: A Grateful Farewell

Thank you for joining us on this journey through a year that holds a special place in our hearts. Whether you experienced 1963 firsthand or through the pages of this book, we hope it brought you moments of joy, nostalgia, and connection to a time that will forever shine brightly in our memories.

Share Your Thoughts and Help Us Preserve History

Your support and enthusiasm for this journey mean the world to us. We invite you to share your thoughts, leave a review, and keep the spirit of '63 alive. As we conclude our adventure, we look forward to more journeys through the annals of history together. Until then, farewell and thank you for the memories.

We would like to invite you to explore more of our fantastic world by scanning the QR code below. There you can easily get free ebooks from us and receive so many surprises.

Copyright EdwardArtLab.com

TO DO LIST

- ○ --
- ○ --
- ○ --
- ○ --
- ○ --
- ○ --
- ○ --
- ○ --
- ○ --
- ○ --
- ○ --
- ○ --
- ○ --
- ○ --

well done!

To Do List

- [ ]
- [ ]
- [ ]
- [ ]
- [ ]
- [ ]
- [ ]
- [ ]
- [ ]
- [ ]
- [ ]
- [ ]
- [ ]
- [ ]

To Do List

- [ ] _____
- [ ] _____
- [ ] _____
- [ ] _____
- [ ] _____
- [ ] _____
- [ ] _____
- [ ] _____
- [ ] _____
- [ ] _____
- [ ] _____
- [ ] _____
- [ ] _____
- [ ] _____

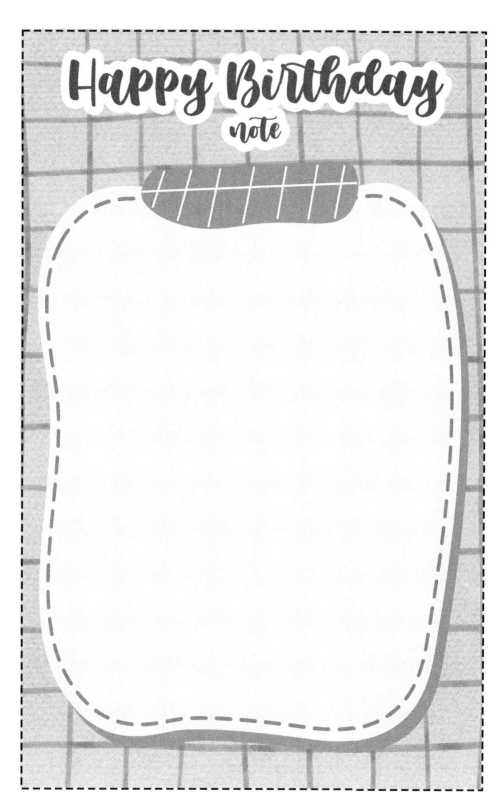

Happy Birthday

note

Happy Birthday

note

HAPPY BIRTHDAY NOTE

TO DO LIST

Name: _____ Day: _____ Month: _____

No	To Do List	Yes	No

TO DO LIST

Name: _____ Day: _____ Month: _____

No	To Do List	Yes	No

TO DO LIST

Name: _____   Day: _____   Month: _____

No	To Do List	Yes	No

NOTE

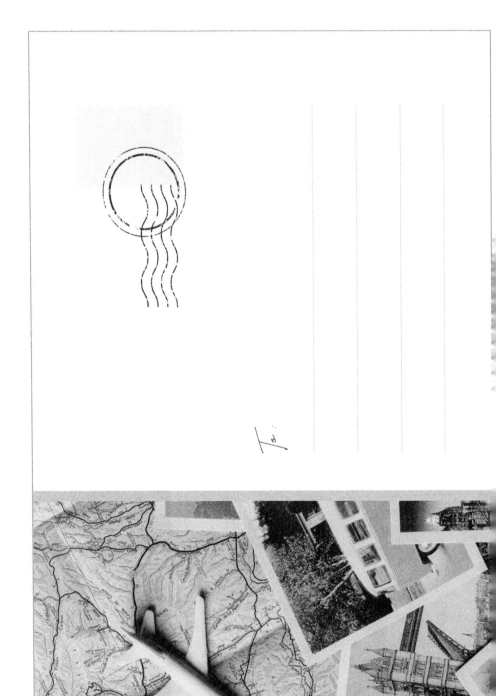

Remember This!

WISH YOU WERE HERE,
123 ANYWHERE ST., ANY CITY

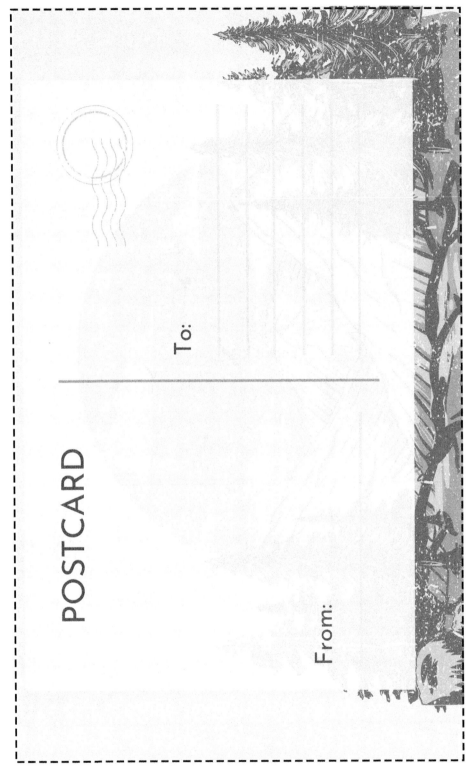

POSTCARD

To:

From:

Printed in Great Britain
by Amazon

33468597R00069